MW00638879

TO DO:

☐ GET DAD'S LIFE
INSURANCE PAYOUT

☐ ENTRUST MOST OF IT TO
SOME GUY TO INVEST IN
A LIQUOR STORE

☐ PROFIT, PROBABLY

INSPIRED BY
A RAISIN IN THE SUN, LORRAINE HANSBERRY

TO DO:

- ☐ BREAK UP WITH OPHELIA

- ☐ AVENGE FATHER'S DEATH

- ☐ TRY NOT TO MURDER ANYONE BY ACCIDENT

INSPIRED BY
HAMLET, WILLIAM SHAKESPEARE

TO DO:

☐ OFFICIATE ROMEO AND
    JULIET'S MARRIAGE

☐ GIVE JULIET THE SLEEPING
    DRAUGHT

☐ BE SURE TO TELL ROMEO

INSPIRED BY
ROMEO AND JULIET, WILLIAM SHAKESPEARE

TO DO:

☐ BUY A MANSION ON
LONG ISLAND

☐ THROW PARTIES FOR
THE WOMAN I LOVE

☐ JUST KIND OF HOPE
SHE SHOWS UP

INSPIRED BY
THE GREAT GATSBY, F. SCOTT FITZGERALD

TO DO:

- ☐ WIN THE TROJAN WAR

- ☐ TAKE A DETOUR TO THE
  ISLAND OF THE CYCLOPS

- ☐ BE HOME BY DINNER

INSPIRED BY
THE ODYSSEY, HOMER

TO DO:

☐ JOURNEY ACROSS THE LAND
OF NIGHT AND THE WATERS
OF DEATH

☐ FIND THE SECRET TO
IMMORTALITY

☐ WATCH OUT FOR SNAKES

INSPIRED BY
THE EPIC OF GILGAMESH, ANONYMOUS

TO DO:

☐ PUSH THE BOULDER UP A HILL

☐ PUSH THE BOULDER UP A HILL

☐ PUSH THE BOULDER UP A HILL

INSPIRED BY
THE MYTH OF SISYPHUS, ALBERT CAMUS

TO DO:

☐ ACCUSE PEOPLE OF
WITCHCRAFT

☐ WATCH SALEM FALL
INTO CHAOS

☐ LEAVE TOWN

INSPIRED BY
THE CRUCIBLE, ARTHUR MILLER

TO DO:

☐ COMMIT MURDER AND HIDE
   THE BODY

☐ ADMIT THE DEED

☐ TEAR UP THE PLANKS TO
   SILENCE THE BEATING OF
   HIS HIDEOUS HEART

INSPIRED BY
"THE TELL-TALE HEART," EDGAR ALLAN POE

TO DO:

☐ DETHRONE THE KING OF SCOTLAND

☐ CIRCLE BACK WITH THE WITCHES

☐ PRESUMABLY HAVE A LONG AND PROSPEROUS REIGN

INSPIRED BY
MACBETH, WILLIAM SHAKESPEARE

TO DO:

☐ PROPOSE TO ELIZABETH

☐ BECOME HUMBLED BY
   REJECTION AND ULTIMATELY
   GROW AS A PERSON

☐ PROPOSE AGAIN

INSPIRED BY
PRIDE AND PREJUDICE, JANE AUSTEN

TO DO:

☐ CREATE A MONSTER WHOSE
VERY EXISTENCE SPITS IN THE
FACE OF THE NATURAL ORDER

☐ REJECT HIM

☐ TAKE A NAP

INSPIRED BY
FRANKENSTEIN, MARY SHELLEY

TO DO:

☐ TRANSFORM INTO A GIANT
INSECT

☐ RUMINATE ON THE TRAPPINGS
OF CAPITALISM

☐ SCUTTLE

INSPIRED BY
THE METAMORPHOSIS, FRANZ KAFKA

TO DO:

☐ FALL IN LOVE

☐ DIE OF A VAGUE ILLNESS

☐ HAUNT HEATHCLIFF

INSPIRED BY
WUTHERING HEIGHTS, EMILY BRONTË

TO DO:

☐ ESCAPE FROM PRISON

☐ FIND THE TREASURE

☐ EMBARK ON A REALLY
   ELABORATE REVENGE PLOT

INSPIRED BY
THE COUNT OF MONTE CRISTO, ALEXANDRE DUMAS

TO DO:

☐ VOW NEVER TO MARRY

☐ MEDDLE IN EVERYONE'S
LOVE LIVES

☐ REFLECT ON HOW GOOD
I AM AT MATCHMAKING

INSPIRED BY
EMMA, JANE AUSTEN

TO DO:

☐ BE FASHIONABLE

☐ REMAIN RICH

☐ MARRY A MAN NAMED ERNEST,
A NAME THAT INSPIRES
ABSOLUTE CONFIDENCE

INSPIRED BY
THE IMPORTANCE OF BEING EARNEST, OSCAR WILDE

TO DO:

- ☐ FIGHT GRENDEL
- ☐ AND GRENDEL'S MOTHER
- ☐ OKAY, FINE, FIGHT THE
  DRAGON, TOO, I GUESS

INSPIRED BY
BEOWULF, ANONYMOUS

STERLING
New York

An Imprint of Sterling Publishing Co., Inc.

STERLING and the distinctive Sterling logo
are registered trademarks of Sterling Publishing Co., Inc.

ISBN 978-1-4549-4489-8

Distributed in Canada by Sterling Publishing Co., Inc.
C/o Canadian Manda Group, 664 Annette Street
Toronto, Ontario, Canada M6S 2C8
Distributed in the United Kingdom by GMC Distribution Services
Castle Place, 166 High Street, Lewes, East Sussex, England BN7 1XU
Distributed in Australia by NewSouth Books
University of New South Wales, Sydney, NSW 2052, Australia

For information about custom editions, special sales,
and premium and corporate purchases, please contact
Sterling Special Sales at 800-805-5489
or specialsales@sterlingpublishing.com.

Manufactured in India

2 4 6 8 10 9 7 5 3 1

sterlingpublishing.com

Text by Courtney Gorter
Design by Christine Heun
Cover by Melissa Farris